Mary Hall Freedom House

True greatness is to serve unnoticed and to work unseen.

3G Publishing, Inc.
3600 Park Lake Lane
Norcross, Georgia 30092
www.3gpublishinginc.com
Phone: 1-888-442-9637

First published by 3G Publishing, Inc. October, 2012

ISBN: 978-0-9854968-2-1

Printed in the United States of America

Our Journey to Freedom

Foreword

You Never Know

You could have never told me my life would be so good. I started using alcohol and drugs when I was 12 or 13 years old. I do remember it felt good and I wanted that feeling all the time. I spent the next 15 years looking for an escape from my reality, daily.

One day, by divine intervention someone said, "You have the right to remain silent". I cannot imagine freedom being taken from me. I had enough fear and common sense to know I could not go that route my life had to change.

No, I didn't go to jail; I went to a probation officer who asked me to give a urine sample and me being from Tuckahoe, asked, why? She said, "to see if you use drugs", and I said yes I do and she almost fell out of the chair. She asked what I wanted to do about it and I asked what was I supposed to do?

Everybody in my family up to this point, in my eyes died using drugs or alcohol. So wasn't that the way of life? Little did I know, God had plans for me and it was not to die, but to live and live abundantly.

22 years later God not only saved my life but also used the same thing I thought would take my life to show people the way of life. God continues daily to give me light to bring light to others in darkness. Over 22 years ago by the grace of God, I was delivered from addiction, the dark life of substance abuse and given the gift of recovery. Being a person in long-term recovery my life has been turned over to help women out of darkness into the marvelous light.

Over 3500 women have crossed the threshold of Mary Hall Freedom House leaving footprints in my heart. Everyone was created with a divine purpose. Women from all lifestyles with unique gifts and talents come to believe and know they can live life and life abundantly without the use of alcohol, drugs and other abuses.

Women walk out of our doors with a relationship with a God of their understanding, restored and renewed, and knowing a day at a time all things are possible.

I'm grateful one of the women who walked through our doors at a time of need has used her gifts and talents to make this book happen. I am forever grateful to her and excited for every sister who put her story in the book.

God bless.

For I know the plans I have for you," declares the Lord, "plans to prosper you and not to harm you, plans to give you hope and a future.
Jeremiah 29:11

Contents

Chapter One

FAMILY

AMY BELL

Family

Having a family is very important for many reasons: they help you when you are down; they see you shed your tears and they are always there for comfort. I appreciate having a great family that is always there through thick and thin. Moreover, when you need a shoulder to cry on when you are at your lowest point in your life they will be there to lift you up. When you have lost everything, they will be there to give you a hand. Therefore, if you have families learn how to respect each other through all of the hard times because no matter what happens, they will always be your family.

Chapter Two

New Mercies

MONICA BETTIS

New Mercies

You showed me new mercies,
You give me strength,
You blessed my soul.

You delivered me, when I was weak,
You placed your loving arms around me,
You kept me when I could not keep myself.

You loved me when I didn't love myself,
You showed me a way out,
You opened doors for me.

You showed me new mercies!

Philippians 4:13

Chapter Three

A Letter from Mom

Elizabeth Bruner

A Letter from Mom

My Dearest Garrett,

There is so much I want to say, yet I am unsure as where to begin. We are traveling down quite a bumpy road with plenty of twists and turns. Since you were born, there have been times that you and I have traveled together as well as times that we have traveled apart. I pray that you know that you have never been alone.

Our Savior, Jesus Christ, has been a present companion in our times of joy, as well as our times of sorrow. It is only through our relationship with Him that we will find calm in the midst of any storm. We are often uncertain of what life will bring, but when we seek Him with all of our hearts, we will always find an indescribably intimate and soul satisfying peace and strength that is incomparable to anything found in this world. I pray that as you read this, you have learned how to know and trust God's voice - that you want nothing more than to follow His call for your life – that you wait patiently, in eager anticipation, as He shapes and forms you and that you embrace your destiny. Know that you are worthy of all things that are pure and good and lovely.

You will always be the sweetest, nicest, most handsome child of God that I will ever know and that Jesus loves you and I love you and that there is nothing you will ever be able to do about that.

Always and Forever,
Mommy
Elizabeth Bruner

Chapter Four

LONG ROADS, SWEET DREAMS...

HEATHER CLEVELAND

Long roads, Sweet dreams...

INTRODUCTION

Broken wings you seen before. See this newfound glory deep in me. Freedom in my hands, clearness of mind. Standing tall, no shame ....The story of me.

PART 1
WHAT AM I...?

Running wild, roughness on my feet, were the bare earth has touch them more than a time or two. Rawness of my heart... I HATE YOU every day. My mind is crazy wild, Running thoughts that make this girl feel like I haven't slept in days...Just running and running...Tough, brave, strong is what I show you ..Broken, scared and weak is what is real... The inside you will never see. Check out my false pride, of my dependence on you...Wow got ya didn't I...You thought I was so cool casting all my bad juju on you.. Wear and tear of my soul...God forgive me this wild child from mom and pop that was kind of there...So here I am this is what you got...Get it for free this misplaced misfit in me.

PART 2
STRONG WOMAN

Broken I was this girl-Trying to find something I lost. An empty hole left in my heart from such an early age Trying to fill the love I needed, Using false put- me- back together again substitute; glues that didn't last long..Was it the father that was never there the addictive thinking already running deep in my veins? I stole, I lied, I used, I drank, I was wrong.... Living crazy being used and using you... A long road where sweet dreams were only dreams.

-Today-

The women I am trying to be. I want to be understanding with boundaries that stand in place. I want to be beautiful were it don't matter what color I paste on my face. The women I'm trying to be. I want to be the mother that kisses all the boo-boos away... I want to be the backbone of my husband. Love, trust and everlasting we're the vows we promised each other forever... The women I'm trying to be.

Look at me today as I walk passed you. I am proud to be me the woman I have become. Strong and focused caring and understanding. Beautiful without vain I stand before you ever changing. This women I trying to be. Were broken I was and now healed I am. Long roads of rough streets have paved this way for my sweet dreams.

Little Hands of Mine
To my Children

The things I've seen please close your eyes to. Look away from the damage and torn life I lead. Be a leader my children and follow the righteous path of sweet dreams. Stand tall my offspring be heard as you speak out into this wide-open space of loud talkers, dark shadows of the ones that want to steal your soul. Do not fear my babies, for the Lord will protect you on your vast walk on his stone path of life. To you all three that came from me live different, live right, live free. Laugh and love be brave and strong. Set your feet steady for the foundation of your journey. I will be there every step of the way for the blood that runs deep in you was taken from me, to my three sons.

Love, Mommy

I'M STILL HERE
TO MY HUSBAND

The man after God I put you first. I look back and think of the last 5 years of our lives honey baby I love only you this path of long talks sweet nights and beautiful days that were shared I also remember the fights the times I told you I hated you when you wouldn't listen you made me cry I asked why you said not what you showed but still I stayed I'm not your mother I will be here I know your hurt I know your scared let me in I'm your best friend I'm your girl I'm your wife I'm by your side no matter what we've loved we've shared we've cried I'm here no matter what we go through we will make it through Gods grace I see you for you strong the vows we shared under Gods eyes we said forever I meant it. I'm staying I love your flaws I love your weaknesses I love you for you ….this is to you the man I care for the man I love the man I see.. The father of my children I see what nobody else sees I live for that smile the long laughs. I AM HERE AND I LOVE YOU EVERYDAY

Last thoughts today, I love me I hope you see it on my face as I smile back at you if someone asked me what I would change in my past I would say nothing the hardships of life have taught me to be strong through God I pray and he lifts me up this is my experience. Strength pushes me to focus on day and move forward I see the light bulb moment in the new comers and this is my hope this is my story these are my thoughts I share them with you willingly and open may you find your bottom and start a new LIVE TO THE FULLEST!

Chapter Five

In this Moment

Kala Conley

In this Moment

So in this moment I'm fighting the fight.
Right now I feel blessed and it is alright.

The Past
I'm learning to deal with the pain.
Every morning I wake up is a new moment gained

Taking this opportunity to make a change I'm walking forward without regretting a thing.

This is my last chance now, I've got to get this right.
I'm doing this now in fighting the fight.
It will be a struggle I know, for the rest of my life but my god is with me and he wont leave my side in this with me - to win the fight!

Chapter Six

My Story

SHAMARION CURTIS

My Story

In my 38 years of living, I've finally come to the realization that everyone has a past. I've come to realize if anyone believes in Christ Jesus, they see old things pass away, and all things become new. We have a choice, either hold on to our past and die or let our past go in order to press on with our future and live. The first step to walking toward the future is to receive forgiveness of the past. This is not the easiest thing to do especially if you do not know how to receive. I am still trying to take the first step. You see, I am where I am today because of one decision I made in the past. You must be careful when making decisions you know are wrong because they can have a lasting effect on you and your future. For the past 13 years, I have endured the repercussions of one wrong act of adultery. The bible tells us the thief cometh not but for to steal and to kill and to destroy. The devil is the thief and he has stolen and destroyed my marriage, my family and my life.

Back in 1998, my husband and I sold marijuana out of our apartment. One morning the police raided our apartment. My husband took the charges for the drugs and got 6 months in jail. While he was incarcerated, I came back to God. I had been unemployed at the time, but I soon found a job and another apartment. Things were going good because my steps where being ordered by God. I worked temporarily for a company called Hartz. It was there that I met him. Looking back, I was so deeply deceived. He came as an angel of light, talking the right talk (the God talk) and I fell for it, hook line and sinker. Don't get me wrong now; I'm not blaming anyone. In the end it was my choice to get involved with him, but the devil had it set up from the beginning. I just could not see it.

I'm one who believes that God sometimes speaks through signs. I can remember one time when God gave me a clear sign through a conversation the man at work and I had. The conversation was far from being Godly. We were flirting with each other in a sneaky kind of way but I was well aware of it. I just could not resist the subtle, but very clear words from this handsome brother who was giving me what I craved the most, attention.

Our relationship made a five-year turn after that one conversation. It did not happen overnight, but gradually from small compromises. I would catch him in so many lies; For instance, the lie about his sister who turned out to be his wife. Yes, he was married as well, with two children, and one on the way. He lived on the south side and I lived on the north side. He would come over after his wife went to work. She worked at night. Shortly after my husband came home from jail, he gave me an ultimatum, either him or my husband. I chose him. I left my husband and children for a married man and his children. That is a decision I have regretted to this day. I got an apartment in the same apartment complex as them, right around the corner as a matter of a fact. I would walk over after his wife went to work. I lived the next five years of my life catering to this married man as though he were my husband and I was his wife. We justified ourselves by keeping the spiritual connection alive. Of course, I dreamed of the day when he would leave his wife and marry me, but somewhere in the back of my mind I knew that would never happen. The relationship came to an end after I found a church where I thought I truly had found God for real. I invited him and he came once. The day he came, I came clean with one of the leaders of the church about the true nature of our relationship. Shortly after, I broke up with him for good. I thought that was the end. Little did I know, it was just the beginning.

I opened my spirit, mind and heart wide to the pastor and this newfound church. I even subjected my son to them, only to find out, after they released me, that it was an occult. Never before in my life had I felt so rejected by God. I had embraced this church with my whole being, only to be kicked out. It felt like God himself had slammed the door in my face. That was the ultimate rejection. I literally felt life leaving my body after the pastor called me and informed me that I was no longer welcomed at the church. He said something about God showing different ones in the church. He said I was operating out of witchcraft and rebellion. I did not understand any of what had just transpired on the phone. In my mother's bathroom, with tear stained eyes, I asked God if he was still with me. He answered me yes by putting a rainbow on the bare white wall I'd looked at so many times before. Again, I literally felt life come back in me.

I've gone through many test and trials but I keep the faith that God is with me. My vision has been obscured as a result of a forty day fast, my children were taken from me, my marriage has come to an end and my psychiatrist has labeled me schizophrenic because I was trying to be honest and told her I could hear and see in the spirit. At times, I have felt like I was going to lose my mind but God has proven Himself to be a Keeper. I find strength and encouragement through His word, and by believing that all things will work out for my good and that greater is he that is in me than he that is in this world. I believe the Lord orders my steps. Gods' thoughts toward me are thoughts of good and not evil. They give me a future, hope and a good expected end.

So, I'm turned in the right direction and I'm about to take that first step toward forgiveness where I will let go of the guilt, shame, and condemnation as God pours out His love and forgiveness. I choose to receive it and be made whole.

Chapter Seven

The Past that will not Determine my Future

Aisha Dixon

The Past that will not Determine my Future

As far back as I can remember, I was a little girl, only four years old to be exact, when it began. I can remember always getting woken up out of my sleep by my uncle, my brother's uncle (we have different dads). I would always wonder why I always had to be the one who got woken up from sleep. Nevertheless, I thought I wasn't old enough to be asking these questions. I can remember turning six years old and the wake ups never stopped. Instead of getting McDonald's for the good things I did, I would get it before I would have to perform sexual acts. I guess that was supposed to be my prize.

The abuse went on and on for several more years. Not only was I going through sexual abuse, I was also going through physical abuse by my mother. She was being abused by my father and stepfather; therefore, she began to abuse us. Beating us upside the head with anything she could get her hands on. We never got to be normal kids because we would never be able to go outside to play. I used to wonder to myself why did I have to have the mean mother unlike everyone else. We stayed with our mother up until I was around eight years old. We were then carted back and forth from my mom's house to Grandma's house and then back to mom's again.

One day I will never forget, it was the fourth of July. My mom took us to get an outfit and we were so happy. What we didn't know was that this would be the last time we would see my mom again for a long time. We all jumped in a cab going to Grandma's not knowing she would kick us out the cab in the middle of the street and tell us to walk the rest of the way. I remember we knocked on Grandma's door and my aunt answered the door asking us what we were crying for. We explained to everybody that our mother dropped us off and told us she would come back and get us later. I remember our aunt looking at us like we were crazy and my grandmother stepping in and saying you all can stay here as long as you need. My grandmother kept us for a couple of years and took care of us like we were her own; even though my brother has a different dad, he stayed too. We stayed in church and lived good until my mother called out of the blue one day saying she wanted her kids back. My grandmother didn't have a choice but to send us to her. She must have finally realized she could not live financially without us as far as welfare.

When we first got there my mother and step father were living in a hotel. I would always remember she would always walk in and out of the room. Why did she do this? My guess is as good as yours. But finally I guess we got a little bit too expensive because we had to end up living with some people we didn't even know who my step dad met through his labor day job. We moved in with them and almost immediately one of the men began to touch me. That went on for a while and I told my mom. She said everybody needed to sleep in the same room from now on. Not that it did any good because that's when I realized my step dad was a child molester, too. I remember him thinking I was asleep and he would climb on the side my sister was on and began to have sex with her. I couldn't do anything but cry because I was scared to say anything. Finally I remember moving to our own home which made matters worse.

When we first got our new house, my step dad ended up going to jail and the only thing my mother was worried about was him. She was so committed to making sure he was all right that we became reliable for ourselves the majority of the time .We would have to cook and clean for ourselves. Not to mention we were also responsible for everything my mother needed done, too. My mother became very lazy and all she did was watch TV and eat. She was probably depressed because my stepfather was gone. We would never be able to go outside to play with the other kids. The closest we got to outside was looking out the window. I believe that's when I began to rebel.

I would start getting in trouble in school. When I would get in trouble, I would get beat, really beat. Anything my mother could get her hands on: shoes, sticks, irons, chairs, anything. She would begin to beat me. I remember when I was thirteen, her getting a boyfriend meant he could abuse me, too. I asked myself why was she prone to men that were sexually abusive? Then when she broke up with him, she let the uncle from when I was a child move back in with us. He was only there for a short period of time. I told my mother what had been going on and she didn't believe me at first until she caught him on top of my sister. She kicked him out of the house finally which was a surprise to me.

The beatings continued up until I was fourteen, by this time my stepfather had gotten out but violated his parole and he died in jail from pneumonia. So the beatings got worse; we began to sneak out of the house because we weren't allowed to see sunlight besides going back and forth from school, doing all the grocery shopping, and other shopping my mother needed to get done. We were her personal slaves. I remember she used to tell us the only way we could go outside was to go and steal her stuff out of the store.

My mother became physically sick; she had a ligament in her back she claimed she couldn't move. But it was funny, she was ok on the first of the month. She started to tell my sister she had to discipline us, my sister was seventeen and I was fourteen at the time. I remember she used to get off of work and if we had done anything bad, my mother would chastise my sister and make her punish us. My sister would beat us the exact same way my mother would and I would hate her for it. She would make us get naked and get in the bathtub with water. I finally got fed up and told my mother I was going to a party next door and I haven't been home since. I will never forget talking to my sister and her telling me I was the weaker one for leaving.

When I turned 18, I was no longer a ward of the state

but I continued to be a victim of the street. I had nowhere to go besides my Aunt's house so I would sleep anywhere else I could when I didn't want to be there. By the grace of GOD, I received Section 8 housing and got my own place.

I had my first child at 16. I was in a foster home and they told me if I completed the program, they would give me my child back but it never happened. They tricked me into signing adoption papers and said it would be an open adoption. Everything changed so I rebelled and ended up running away from the group home and committed crimes like robbery, theft, car theft, and credit card misuse. I ended up serving 15 months in a Juvenile Detention Center. I got a couple of visits when I first got there but that was it.

Back to when I was 18, I got my own home and that was when I got pregnant with my second child. I had the child and ended up pregnant with my third child. I ended up moving back to Georgia and everything went downhill from there. I sent my second child back up north and my using of drugs progressed.

I was introduced then to Ecstasy pills and my life really spun out of control. I started drinking more and began to sell my body. I went back up north to visit and got pregnant again by my second child's father. I came back south with the baby and I continued to use more and more. When I had my fourth child, I was leaving the kids anywhere I could so I could run the streets and continue to get high. I had my fifth child and by that time my using had progressed even more. I was sent to rehab and my kids had to stay with their God family until I finished rehab. I finished rehab and got my kids back, but my mind was still on doing the same old habits. By that time, I was introduced to cocaine while in the rehab system so I had to go become an outpatient. While as an outpatient, I would only use on the weekend so my system would be clean by the time the next week came.

I got pregnant again and had my sixth child while in the midst of being an outpatient for rehab, I continued to use and had a seventh child. I attempted to get married but I stayed high so much I couldn't even function enough to get my paperwork together. I moved to another neighborhood thinking everything would change. By that time, I was pregnant with my eighth child and I was still using. Things had gotten even worse then before. I moved to another new home, which by this time, it had been the third move in the same neighborhood. I kept blaming the condition of the house for the reason I had to move over and over again but it was just an excuse for me to use. I used the rent money to get high.

I was in a relationship with my child's father. I'm pregnant now with his child. This is number nine and I had to really sit down and take a look at my life and realize I had lived all my life as a lie. I was homeless in a rooming house paying by the week with hardly any food and still prostituting to get what I needed. Thirty years old with eight kids and pregnant with nothing to show. How could I ever expect a man to ever respect me when I didn't even respect myself? How would I ever have a relationship with my kids? How would I ever have a stable home or marriage or ever a higher power if I were stuck in bondage? I prayed that GOD would just send an angel to come rescue me, and on January 13, I entered Mary Hall and I've been clean 26 days. Now that I'm closer to my higher power, things have become very clear to me. All the mistakes I have made. I've forgiven those who have hurt me. I've forgiven my mom; I love her with all my heart and I want to have the best relationship with my kids I can have. I also want to get closer to the Lord and live the way he intended me to live. I'm not perfect but I'm getting better each day.

Chapter Eight

A New Beginning

Stephanie Duffey

A New Beginning

I am Stephanie Duffey, a client at Mary Hall Freedom House. I have been attending Mary Hall Freedom House for 30 days now. I am now 26 years old and have been facing the addiction of meth for the last 12 years.

Mary Hall freedom House is my first rehab that I have ever attended. I wanted to come to rehab to better myself and find out who the real Stephanie is. This has been a wonderful experience so far and I am proud to be here and very thankful.

Before I went to jail in December, I lost complete custody of my daughter, Brynlee, in October of 2011. That was the worst day of my life. I don't think I ever shed so many tears over a person. I felt that my heart was ripped out of my chest and it would never be replaced. Having to sign the papers that day created a hurt and hate for myself. After lying in the bed and crying for days, I went back out and started getting high once again. I wanted to numb the pain I was feeling. Dope was doing that for me at the time. I was high for the next month. I had been up for 7 days with no sleep at all when I went to jail in December. I caught my first possession charge of meth and marijuana and a pipe charge as well. At that time, what I thought dope was numbing was really not letting me face reality. I then realized in jail when I was sobering up that dope has done nothing for me in life but ruin it for me.

I knew then I was done being sick and tired. I wanted help, I wanted treatment, I wanted my family back, and I wanted to be sober for my daughter. I fell on my knees one night begging for forgiveness and asking God for the strength to help me overcome my addition. I was ready to change and most importantly, I wanted to change. After I prayed and cried that night, I started seeing him answering my prayers one by one. I knew it was time for me to enter treatment. My spirit was starting to rise more and more every day. God was not going let my probation pull my 15 months that I had left and God is going to help me get my daughter back. I knew not to worry about Floyd County and his 15 months because God had bigger and better plans for me.

Now that I am at Mary Hall Freedom House, I know that I will finally get the treatment and the help with my addition that I have wanted for the last 12 years of my life. I am taking classes for my GED as well and working toward it. I am so thankful for this program and what it has to offer me. I am learning so much here and could not ask for a better opportunity than this. I also know that if you don't want the help then you will never receive it until you are truly ready for it. I am truly ready to change and become a better person, but not only for myself but also for my 6-year-old daughter, Brynlee, which is out there depending on me in life to guide her, protect her and LOVE her. I know in my heart that I will regain custody back of her and be here once again and never lose that. I am here to say that dope is not worth it and never has been.

I want to say thank you to all the people that have supported me at Mary Hall Freedom House and to my family for all the prayers and support.

Chapter Nine

NOTHING LED ME TO YOU

JESSIE EATON

Nothing Led me to You

Riding down the rapids.
On my way to sea.
Tumbling over rocks.
Struggling to find me.
Lost among the chaos.
Grasping at the sky.
Holding onto nothing,
but a handful of lies.

Where's my inspiration?
Is there anyone to call?
Faith leads me to arms,
open to catch me fall.
Suddenly I am thrown,
into deadly calm,
able to catch my breath,
and open up my palms.

Reaching up to Heaven,
screaming out His name,
Praying for forgiveness,
and release from the pain.
Bring me to the light.
Reveal the path to take.
Lead me to salvation,
and redemption when I wake.

I see You stand before me.
My eyes are open wide.
The past is all receding.
I've nothing left to hide.

A new beginning awaits.
I'm reaching for Your hand.
Walking in the footsteps,
planted in the sand.

Show me all Your glory,
so I can spread The Word.
When all I had was nothing,
it was Your voice that I heard.

Chapter Ten

Light after Dark

Hillary Hammond

Light after Dark

DEDICATED TO MY CHILDREN
JAKOB, JAMES AND LUKAS

I've endured many challenges been through so much I was
so broken so out of touch the road I went down was stripping
my soul there was no beat in my step no more life in my flow
there was good news but I couldn't hear it I was consumed
with sin and drugs were breaking my spirit I was so lost my
will was weak God knew where I was all I had to do was seek I
didn't know who I was I lost my place God saved me with his
wonderful amazing grace I've felt so much hurt I cried in pain
God gave me hope he gave me peace to maintain Good news
you shall rap in joy what you sow in tears there is still struggles
in life God can help with fears don't ever stop your journey
continue your quest let God guide you and your Path will be
blessed just remember you are not a prodigal of your past God
can cleanse you, restore you if you only ask.

Chapter Eleven

SANITY

Jennifer Ingram

Sanity

I want to dedicate my story to my family who has been there for me through it all, the good, the bad, and the ugly. I am Jennifer Ingram, a recovering alcoholic and addict. I have been in and out of recovery most of my adult life. I am 38 years old. I started drinking at 16 years old. From the start, I was at the least, an abuser. By age 17, I was in my first rehab center. I didn't take anything seriously at age 17; there were not many things that I did take seriously. I summed that experience up to things I shouldn't do next time to keep from getting caught drinking. That was the beginning of my fight with alcoholism. I didn't realize it then. I do realize it now. For the next few years, my alcoholism began to get more and more real to me.

I also began fighting depression. I would use the alcohol to numb out the depression. Then, I would get myself into more trouble for drinking so much. I would become even more depressed with the problems compounding. I would drink even more next time to numb out even more depression and loneliness. This cycle would continue for several years. I tried everything, changing from alcohol to any and all other kinds of mind-altering substances. It would always lead me back to alcohol and depression. Over and over and over again, round and round I went in a vicious cycle. All the guilt, shame and anger that I had inside me was killing me. I didn't know how to handle it. It just grew and grew until it was a monster in my life and in my mind. A monster, so strong, that I didn't know how to fight it. Over the years, I came to believe that I was powerless over drugs and alcohol and my life was unmanageable. My next obstacle was coming to believe that a power greater than myself could restore me to sanity. In my home, there wasn't any spirituality. Growing up, there was never talk of a higher power. If I couldn't see it, I didn't believe it existed. Then I started trying to put more thought into it. I started thinking about love and the fact that I can't see it, I can't touch it, and I can't taste it. I know it is there because I can feel it in my heart. If I look for it, I can see evidence of it. Soon after that, I found out God is love and you have to receive him on a daily basis to combat the monsters and demons in your life.

The depression, the guilt, and shame of all the things in my past, God is the answer. God is love. Today I can feel his love in my heart; I can see the evidence of him in my life. I look for him and seek him every day on the good days, the bad days and on all the in between days. My family is still together after all these years. My children are wonderful. My son is an awesome hunter and fisherman. His grades could very well get him a scholarship for college. My daughter is a good student. She is a star softball player and an award-winning gymnast. Their father has never given up on me. He continued loving me through all these years. He loved me when I didn't love myself. He took care of our beautiful children when I could not. He has never lost faith in me and I have never lost faith in him. True love will overcome all.

Last, but certainly not least, my parents are the backbone of all our lives. When all else failed, they were there to keep our family together. They were there to take the kids to ball practice and doctor's appointments when we could not. They saved our house from being foreclosed. Whatever we needed that we did not have, for one reason or another, they were there for us all. I love my whole family for sticking together through it all. When I see others who along the way of addiction, have lost it all and completely alone. Through the mercy and grace of God, I have:

S- Strength

A – Acceptance

N- New life

I – Integrity

T – Trust

Y – Yes, my higher power

I have made it to Mary Hall Freedom House.

Chapter Twelve

TEMPTATION

LaTandra Jones

Temptation

Surrounded by plenty of people
voices are shouting and sound angry
my thoughts are unable to be heard
my lips are moving with no sound to words
everybody else is doing it
that's what they are all saying
just try it once you will be ok
looking around they seem happy
I wanna be happy too
moving my hands to try it once
inhale, exhale, coughing real hard
 start to feel numb and real good
all the heartache and pain gone
once turned to twice and twice turned to thirty
now strung out just to be cool
doing it every day without a care in the world
well that right there was my last
cause that was the old me in the past

STICKY RASPBERRY YOGURT
it's a hot summer's day
all the kids are at play
tried to go swimming for fun
but it didn't help with the sun
coming in the house for air
sweat dripping down my hair
looking in the fridge for something to eat
its right in my face and it smells so sweet

Chapter Thirteen

I Made It!

Jeanne Knox

I Made It!

I grew up in fear, doubt and low self esteem. My family history consists of addiction, depression, poverty and struggle from my great grandparents on both sides and on down the family line. I lived through four deaths in my family as a result of alcohol abuse. I was raised by my mother and then by my aunt. My mother was short tempered and dealt with no nonsense. I was scared to say the wrong thing, look the wrong way, and scared my sister would do something wrong. I never seemed to get it right, so I stayed quiet and out of sight.

When my sister and I stayed with my aunt, it was about church and raising her children. I wasn't allowed to do anything "worldly" that included having friends or going to functions outside of church. I never really learned social skills. I was either too afraid or not allowed. When my mother died, I was 15. I felt abandoned again. I wasn't worth living for or loving so I gave up. I put effort into absolutely nothing, so I dropped out of school, moved hours away to a Job Corps and there, is where I found acceptance with other kids going through similar circumstances. There is also, where I was introduced to drugs and alcohol. For the first time I felt "normal". My disease was progressive from using to abusing then becoming dependent on alcohol.

I have two teenage boys that are truly ride or die. They've been through the good and the bad but always at my side, always showing loveand defiantly voicing their concerns. When they were younger, they were my motivation, the reason I woke up in the morning, worked, did what I had to do to support us. But as my addiction progressed, I was basically on auto pilot- emotionally disconnected. I was still missing something so I continued with the best filler I knew and that was drinking. Divine Intervention- God knows how to reach me.

A series of events occurred that awakened the denial. After being evicted, my children and I were in a shelter and got kicked out because of my drinking. From then on we were staying with one relative to other. Within a month's time I was locked up twice. The second time I spent the day in jail on my mother's birthday. That triggered the thought of my mother's death from alcohol poisoning when my sister and me were around the same age as my children. Thinking of the pain, abandonment, and blame I felt and lived with caused me to think of how I was stealing my children's happiness. If I continue this path, I will die and my children will suffer the same hurt.

I absolutely cannot do this by myself. I am tired and scared. God I do not want to die; I want a better life for my boys, and me and I want to feel joy and peace. HE heard me and Mary Hall Freedom House was where God placed me. The void, the hole in my life I tried so desperately to fill, has been filled with God's love. It sounds good, pretty generic., This is something that normally wouldn't come from these lips except for the fact that I'm actually experiencing it. I'm talking and seeing HIM move mountains in my life, doing what no man or even my imagination could dream up. HE's even giving me the sight to notice HIM moving in my sisters at Mary Hall. I pray for us all the time so God can give the ladies abundance in all areas of our lives and that we recognize and give him the glory. No fear no worry- I can do all things because I got that super natural on my side, the Father, Son and The Holy Ghost. A "survivor" is what I called myself keeping my head above water, getting my ass kicked but still breathing. Now, I call myself a "soldier," fighting back the advisory, arming myself with tools and letting God handle the rest. Today, I contend to the army of the Lord .

I knew my destiny as a struggle. There was not much hope there-motivation was nonexistent. Was I angry with God? Yup. He knows all, right? Right. How I would grow up, who and where I would be raised, the struggles, the pain- thanks a lot. Today, I really thank Him, the way I see it the "experiences, molding and grooming." All the ups and downs are to qualify me for His purpose for my life. I still have some struggles but today I know I'm not alone and I will be successful when I do the next best thing and I stay on Gods side.

A Love Note to my boys, my sister and family: Thank you for seeing the potential in me, and never giving up on that one day. You will have the mom/sister/cousin that you'd be proud of. The time has come y'all. We always knew there was something special about this family and I found out it was God always having HIS hand on us. Joy and abundance is coming our way sayeth the Lord. Yup, that's what HE told me. Stay on HIS team, continue to thank HIM and give HIM the praise. The battle is the Lord's. We never have to stay stuck. Love you so much, xoxoxoxo.

Chapter Fourteen

A Vision of Desire

Barbara Lumpkin

A Vision of Desire

Yes, I'm still here. Where are you?
Right here. Where is here?
Peace be still It's dark, I can't see!
What was once a sweet melody of peace to my ears,
now is spooky sounds of Goons and Goblins.
It sounds like vicious animals are ready to tear me apart.
how did I get here?

Where am I supposed to start?
I pinched myself—Damn it's real!!!!!
I'm now in darkness quite and still.
My heart echoes my sound of sight.
follow a trail that has snares and stumbling blocks.
I fall, I roll try to dip. My head carry knots.
My heart is the biggest lump of all.
I walk down this path with scrapes and bruises.
My soul is a well that has run dry.
But my spirit tells me I must try.
My eyes fail me with sight because I'm blinded with tears.
How do I let go of my chest chambers of fear?
I continue down this path that fails me in desire.

This road has to guide me to a place that is higher.
I use my senses even though I can't see
I open my hands that I may feel
I hold myself tight to ease my fear
What is inside is yet to my surprise, I feel a beat
That is full of desire tempered in heat.
On this ground I walk with my feet
knowing that with this walk, I'm still not in self defeat
I smell a sweet smell of victory,
and follow the glimmer of light

to let me know everything is alright.
I continue to grow along my path
a bright image of life.
Now I see myself
I'm found as life in sight

Chapter Fifteen

SOMETHING ABOUT MY LIFE

DELORES MURRAY

Something About my Life

You think that the high will solve all of your problems, but it really doesn't. The high just medicates the problem and then you have two problems. You start with a drug problem then you just add more problems. By the grace of God, I am learning how to deal with life on life's terms. I knew I needed to find a treatment center and that place is Mary Hall Freedom House. Here, I learn how to deal with life on life's terms. I want to live for God and myself again. I will tell everyone I can, "Don't self medicate any problem." Talk about your problems. Don't keep it all inside because, for me, I kept all my problems inside. I would tell myself it's my problem and I'm stuck with it. I turned to alcohol and drugs and it just got worse. I needed more and more. I started to get depressed and wanted to kill myself. I stopped loving myself and turned away from my family to make them happy. That just made me sink in to self-pity.

I wanted to know why no one loved me. I just wanted to be loved. My kids seemed to love me only for what I can give them. When I did not give something to my kids, they just got mad. So I said to the Lord, "What have I done for them to treat me like a doormat?"

My husband doesn't care about my recovery. When I was clean, he and my nephew drank every day. Even when I told him that the drinking was getting to me, and it was a problem, they don't care. They only care about themselves. I also lost my kids over eight years ago because of my drug problem. It was hard for me when they came back because they don't look at me as their Mom. I did my best to show them how much I love them. But they didn't want to be in my life. Then I lost the focus on me and put it on them. But that was the wrong thing to do. I started buying their love by giving them anything just for them to love me. Then I turned to drink to kill the pain just for a minute. I also started to smoke crack cocaine. The only people who care about me were two little kids, my granddaughter Daisa and my nephew Japaris. Then I let them down when I stopped spending time with them, stopped calling them. If it were not for these two kids, I would have killed myself. I thought about just how much I would have hurt them two kids. I was still hurting so I let the drug take me away from them.

Today I am in treatment to find myself so I can love myself again. I don't care if no one loves me today. As long as God loves me and I love myself, it's about me today. Don't use any drugs because the HIGH is a LIE.

"THE HIGHER POWER"

Life was too hard and I couldn't help but feel hopeless and even suicidal. I felt suicidal, but something inside of me made me not want to give up. Then life happened and something out of my control happened bringing me down. But I hung on knowing that I needed help. GOD came to help me to get back up! GOD gave me hope!

"THE MAN WITH MANY FACES"

Once upon a time, I met a man with many faces. He told me that he would love me to the end of time. He brought me a gift. I ask him, "What is this?" He told me a gift of love. I asked again, "What is this?" Again, he told me a gift of love, joy and happiness. I asked, "How do you know?" He responded saying, "Do I look happy and at peace? Just try it." I asked, "What do you call it?" He replied, "Crack cocaine - a friend to the end." I did try it, and it felt SO GOOD. Oh yes it is a friend to the end. I felt love, happiness, peace and joy.

I was so in love with this gift. Then the man said, "Do you really love my friend?" "Oh yes" I said. "Just only me and my friend crack cocaine." He ask, "So you don't want anything or anybody but me?" I asked, "What about my family?" He said, "I am your family now". "What about my respect? Do you need it or a home?" he asked. "Oh then I just have you and your gift." I said. "Yes my love, you do have to give up your family, friends and my respect. My gift would take all of that away anyway." He said soothingly.

I know one thing, and that is all my love for "GOD" he is the best gift that I have ever had. He gives me happiness and real Love - unconditional. Not like your gift. I just have to keep the faith, hope, and belief in my Heavenly Father. He loves me more every day. He only has one face and that is Love. You have many faces. GOD gives me many choices, and many gifts. His gifts cover me in Love. Your gift, man, is the gift of HATE! I had to pay a High price for your gift – in order to be happy. GOD just gives me my only choice, already paid for by the blood of Jesus Christ. He is there when I think he isn't. GOD will always Love me to the end.

Chapter Sixteen

METH

MARY SHANTEL NEESE

My Story About Meth

My name is Mary Shantel Neese (Breed). I will start by saying meth is also known as crank and ice. It is something I would never in my life ask anyone to try. One time is all it takes most of the time. It is one of the deadliest drugs you could ever do. And believe me, I know because I'm a victim of it for 20 years.

I started off eating meth at the age of 20. I was around people that was doing it. I had never seen this drug in my life. Anyway, the first time I laid eyes on this hell bound drug was with my ex-sister-in-law. We were driving cars from Georgia to Alabama. We had to get up about 5 am to start that morning. I was very tired because I really wasn't an early bird; I was more of a night person. Anyway, I just could not get awake and I had a very bad headache so Tanya came to me with this white powder and said open your mouth. Well I did and she poured this stuff in my mouth and it was awful tasting but not too long after that, I was up awake and ready to work. I never thought I would get hooked. From there on out I was, like I said, 20 years worth of addiction. So here I am 20 years old, with 2 babies at that time, Candy and Brandy, and their mother was hooked on a drug.

Well, I had no job to support my babies, let alone an addiction. What was I thinking? Not nothing but how I was going to get my next bag. I never thought about my babies or my family I was hurting. And not for one minute did it cross my mind about them (my kids) when they were old enough they would also do the same drug and also be addicted but all these years they had seen their mother do this so, to them it was ok. Well my oldest daughter wised up and got her life in order. My middle daughter is getting her life in order after she lost her oldest baby, served time in State Prison, and has liver Cancer. I have lost not only a grand baby but my youngest daughter because of this hell bound drug called meth. Today I have gotten my life together by the grace of God. I have hurt everyone in my family all these years. My mom is 64 years old and through all this, she had never turned her back on me. She is a great woman and very strong. I can't ever go back and change what I did or the ones I hurt. All I can do is go forward and keep living my life as a changed person. I never want to live that over again. I basically lost everything. I lost my whole family, I lost my little girl and grand baby, my husband, whom I am very much in love with, is now in jail. He also has changed his life for the good and I am working on getting my youngest daughter back with me. I have a wonderful mother-in-law, Merina. She has also stood by me from the start. I have to thank all my family for all their support. I am changed today, one day at a time.

So here's a message to all that read this: Don't let the drug called meth send you to hell because it takes full control and destroys lives. And it hurts everyone and everything you love. Today I have turned my life over to a Higher Power, The Lord. I was at the end because I was using needles, something I said I would never do.

I just want to thank everyone for giving me a chance for a new life. First, my Lord, my family, and the Mary Hall Freedom House staff and Ms. Lucy.

Thank you all.

My Kids & Grand kids
Candy, Brandy, Lacy and Grand babies
Mother & Husband Margaret and Lee
Mother-in-Law Merina
And most of all the Lord and Ms. Lucy of
Mary Hall Freedom House
My Counselor Ms. Erica
Case Worker Ms. Bonner

Chapter Seventeen

My Journey Can Only Get Better

Natasha Nix

My Journey Can Only Get Better

My name is Natasha Nix. On November 10th, I was born in a small town known as Brunswick Georgia, at Memorial Hospital. My parents were Mark Nix and Deborah Bell Nix. I had a brother named Charles Nix who was three years older than me. I don't remember much of my childhood. What I do remember was pretty violent. My parents were married but I can't say happily. My father was very abusive mentally and physically to my mother. They both drank alcohol at the time. Looking back now, I know they were alcoholics. He would come home all the time drunk accusing her of cheating on him when he was the only one who was out. She was home caring for my brother and me. It caused me a lot of depression and low self esteem. I can remember my brother, my mom and me came home and my father had broken everything in the house and spray painted bad things about my mom all over the walls. That was the breaking point to what ended their marriage. I was about five years old at this time.

After the divorce, I can remember sitting on the couch with my mother and she was crying her eyes out. I was wondering why she could not be happy with just my brother and me. The depression had a lot of effect on me as a child. My house turned into a party pad for who ever wanted to join. Drinking and drugging was all that existed. As I got older I, felt like I could join and I knew they would not remember the next day. My mom would black out on the regular. My brother and I took advantage of that. We became very impulsive and reckless. We would steal their cars and have them back in the driveway the next morning and get ready for school as if nothing had happened. There was many times my mom felt stupid because my brother and I would tell her some of the things that happened the night before, in hopes that she would quit. It never worked!

As a child, I spent a lot of time at my Grandmother- Mary Woodard's house who lived around the block. And beside her was my mom's sister, Roxanne, who was married to Steve Rhymes. There was my cousin, Christina Rhymes, who was the same age as me. We were like sisters. I had no other sibling besides my brother. We would play and always had a good time. At their house, I learned there is a lot more to the drug scene. My aunt and uncle would always sit in the kitchen and we children could not go through the kitchen. I can remember seeing them with belts tied around their arms and needles sticking out. At the time, I did not realize what they were doing. But I felt it was bad because they would be standing straight up asleep, or using the restroom asleep. There was blood splats on the ceiling from them pulling the needles out of their arms. I can remember they had so much marijuana that you could not even walk into the bedroom.

It wasn't long they started hallucinating, thinking they were seeing monkeys swinging through the trees. They had believed this to be so true they started walking around the yard with loaded shotguns and binoculars asking me and my cousin, "did you see the same things?" We were convinced that they were seeing this so we agreed. Later one afternoon I jumped on my bike and rode fast as I could to my house. I was riding so fast in fear of these monkeys. When I got home my mom's boyfriend Bobby Anderson was sitting on the steps drinking a beer. I had told him what was going on at my aunt's house. He then told me they were high and were seeing things that were not there.

Chapter Eighteen

How Drugs can Dictate Your Life

Audrey Leann Page

How Drugs can Dictate Your Life

Well my name is Audrey. A little briefing of me is, I am 22 years old. I have a one and a 2 year old and I'm currently 8 months pregnant. I have used drugs since the age of 13. It all started with marijuana and feeling on top of the world. By 16, I was doing cocaine and had a great life, or so I thought. At 18 I suffered a severe heartache with a person, who I thought I deeply loved, left me. My world felt over. So, I moved to a different county. In this county, on this particular road, there was nothing but lowlifes. This was where I got arrested the first time. After a week or two, I started drinking heavily and found myself as low as the people I surrounded myself by. Soon I was arrested again, same charges, same road, and the same month. Once I was released the next day, I tried crack for the first time. I got sick the first and second time I did it but I continued to use. It went from drinking to smoking crack all day. This is where my life started taking a turn for the worse.

My teenage years really didn't mean anything because I could use without consequence. Keep in mind I used marijuana everyday and cocaine very heavily also. Okay, back to the story at hand. So it's still the same month; time goes by slow when you're hardly in your mind. So, I find myself in jail once again, same charges, and the same month. After I got out once again I met a 16 year old guy. I immediately fell for him. It must have been fate.

I packed my stuff to move to the farm but I ended up back in jail for the same charges, the same month, and the same place. Ugh, my life seems to be stuck in this cycle. I got out three days later. I returned to the farm where I immediately felt like home. The farm was a 100-year-old farmhouse on 200 acres of land containing four fishing ponds and cows; it was just perfect.

This 16 year old changed my life. I stopped smoking crack and I didn't drink like I used to. I cooked, cleaned, and took care of my man, his father, and his sister. I had a beautiful simple life. I found out I was pregnant but 8 weeks later I had a miscarriage. I just let it go, unlike the stillborn I experienced at 17 from heavy cocaine use. I won't dwell on that story; there's too many details, too much pain, too many tears, too much everything. So once the farm fell, the 16 year old, now 17 years old, moved in with my grandparents and me. We shall call him Joe. Once again, I was pregnant. My life was great because I had a good man, a baby, and a family. I had completely quit drinking and smoking. I still dabbled with cocaine before my pregnancy. I did however still smoke weed.

I suffered several break ups with Joe until my daughter was born. When she was three months, he left. He left permanently after many heartaches in between. This is where I really stopped being a mother to my daughter. I soon met another man. We met hanging around crack heads, pill poppers and dopers. Well seeing as I came out of a long loving relationship, my emotions got the best of me. I fell in love with him. When my daughter was four months old I found out I was pregnant with my second child at 20 years old. He seemed to be such a good man. He treated me like a queen; he spoiled me. We smoked the finest green and had a seemingly perfect life. He sold drugs and I did drugs. Come to find out that my so-called dream man had warrants out for his arrest. He ended up in jail when I was 7 months pregnant. He got out a week before my son's birth. My son and I tested positive for marijuana. This is where my first DEFACS case began. I stopped smoking weed for three weeks and they dropped the case.

When my son was about a month and a half old, his father returned to jail. I happily moved my son, my daughter, and myself to my grandparents' home. He got out on Aprils fools day. We moved out in a search for jobs. I left my daughter with my grandmother. He went straight back to selling weed which quickly advanced to meth. I tried it my life went spiraling downwards fast and hard. Three weeks went by and I was still awake and cared for nothing but getting high and selling. Each day we went out to sell drugs we had to wait on the police that was watching sitting in front of us every morning. Due to the fact, he was wanted once again. This was our daily lives when we were up those three weeks. I cared not for myself for my son and definitely not my daughter. Exactly a month he was out he ended up in jail once again the judge gave him three years I was lost. I had my son with me but had no idea how to function balancing being high selling an being a parent. My grandmother came and took him form me while I was running the streets. I called the law and the law called defacs due to my deteriorating disposition. DEFACS caught me the morning after the first time I slept in three weeks. They told me to stay at my grandparents for a week until they decided what to do, I refused, I didn't wanna fight and argue I wanted to get high and do what I wanted. I should have stayed needless to say now. They were placed in foster care and I was kicked out of my grandparent's house.

Three days later, I was arrested. I waited six months to start my defacs plan. My case is almost a year now. I found Mary Hall Freedom House, where I met one of my best friends now. Learned I do have hope again I realized my life is great and was taught how to live again without drugs. I have been clean almost a hundred days now. I have no defacs case with my third child. Completed my legal problems with a year's probation and is very close to getting my other two back. Lessons learned secrets keep, there is life beyond drugs and when you lose all sense of hope and yourself just hang on its going to be a long hard wild ride but it's worth every little bit of it. Enjoy the small things in life don't take anything for granted. And if you are at Mary Hall you came to the right place, that has saved my life and many others and have helped myself and many others, restore faith in ourselves. PS, WELCOME TO THE REAL WORLD!

Chapter Nineteen

DESPERATELY SEEKING DENISE

DENISE PARKER

Desperately Seeking Denise

An unwanted child cursed by her father, a little girl that didn't grow up with love. A little girl whose world was turned upside down, tormented in chains for years, carrying her daddy's curse's upon her. A little girl who stopped growing at the age of, well really she didn't know any little girl whose life was completely changed by trauma, drama, you name it. This little girl was confused, being abused and could tell no one. She grew up with all of that hate and bitterness inside her. She was angry at God for allowing it to happen to her. She often wanted to run away or just die. She had to face another day being beaten and tormented all over again. She had to face another day, listening to how black and ugly she was and that she was never going to amount to anything. One day my father took it upon himself to rape me. So, guess what? I totally shut down. Stop growing and started running...

That little girl didn't grow up for a long time. The incident, about three weeks later my father died. My Heavenly father had been trying to reach me but I was unreachable. This little girl grew up in an adult's body but she was still lost and still that little girl. I ran and I ran and I ran some more, until I ran into men who were just like my father. Abused, neglected and abandoned, I always felt neglected and abused by everyone I knew because that's all I've known. I thought by a man beating me, cussing me out meant he loved me, that's all I knew. Until one day I was introduced to my Heavenly father, I remember laying on my bed around 1996-1997. Bro. Wilson prayed and I followed his prayer and I was saved, so I thought. I remember wanting to save the world but the world chewed me up and spit me out. Soon after being saved, I was still using crack, prostituting, whoring and stealing. I was lying and a cheat. Until one day around 2000, I became real sick and the doctors told me I was going to die and I said the devil is a liar.

Revelation

Man's version says I will die, God's says you shall live and not die. My natural father said I was black, ugly, and skinny. My heavenly father says that I am fearfully and wonderfully made and that I am the apple of his eye.

God's Beautiful Creation

I looked out my window one morning and I saw two beautiful birds both were black and white with red beaks and I said to myself, "Wow, look at God's beautiful creations." I looked in the mirror and said, "Wow, look at another beautiful creation of God in me." God doesn't make junk so I've learned God says he hand knitted me in my mother's womb. I realized God has been there for me all along, I just didn't know at the time. Now that I know, I allow his love to flow in my heart and in my life.

I have Hope

When I see myself now I have hope that little girl in me has hope. She is happy and she gets sad, but she rejoices because she has hope for tomorrow because she has met Jesus when no one believed in her. She has hope because she believes in Jesus. She has hope she can love today without expecting anything in return. She cries because she has hope. She can sing hallelujah because she has hope. She can love her enemies because she has hope. She has something to live for. She has hope she is not going to give up today. She has hope. Thank you Jesus. Jesus loves me.

What do you do?

When you have no friends, you have gone on to the bitter end. What do you do when you don't know how to love?

Thank God, he sent his holy spirit by a dove. What do you do when you are left all alone? It's a spiritual song, What do you do when that special someone comes along?. I thank God he has finally come. A little girl cursed as a child but only for a little while. Hey little girl agreeing with God's opinion of me, do I agree with Gods opinion?

Being Me

It's okay if you don't like me. It's okay if you don't like the way I look. It's okay if you don't like the way I talk or if you don't think I'm a quality person. It's okay … It's okay if you don't think I am worthy. It's okay if I disagree with you. It's okay, I still love you. It's not going to change what God sees in me, it's okay.

My Attitude

Excuse me but I have a right to be myself. Excuse me I have a right to express myself; excuse me but I have a right to my own opinions. Excuse me I have a right to use my faith. Excuse me I choose to agree with what God says about me. I value myself today and now you may be excused.

One of a Kind

I thank God for making me just the way I am. God made me for his own purpose. God has taken everything that tormented me to heal me so that I can give him the glory. God has turned my life around for my good; God has turned my life completely around for his good and his glory …Hallelujah…God's masterpiece, I am truly art. God has created me, uniquely, especially from his image and glory..

Am I my Brother's Keeper?

Am I responsible for my brother? Does God hold me

responsible for my brother? I have love for my brother, like no other, but what if your brother doesn't want to receive your help or your love? Do you give up? NO! You just keep praying. Love conquers all. **AMEN**

STAY IN YOUR LANE

Father, God I have to learn to stay in my lane. No matter what comes my way, keep holding straight. I have experienced pain from going into someone else's lane. You will wreck if you are not paying attention to your lane. Keep my eyes on the road is what I have been told. Even though you are surrounded by this world, stay grounded in the word. Stay focused. **AMEN**

WHAT DO YOU DO?

When nobody knows
When you feel like no one cares
What do you do when you reach out
and nobody reaches back?
When no one shows compassion
What do you do when God passes you?
Do you grab hold of God's hand or do you just stand?
When God came my way, I decided not to go astray
And keep holding on to God's unchanging hand.
AMEN

GOD TOOK MY HAND

God took my hand, picked me up
and kissed my cheek and said:
"Hey little girl, I am your heavenly dad.
Don't cry, say goodbye to your past.
I am here and I will never leave you
nor forsake you.
I promise you.

So don't feel blue just know
I will always love you."
AMEN

WHY ARE WE NOT KEEPING IT REAL!

To be a believer in Christ is like being converted, changed, new way of life, new attitude, and a renewed mind in Christ.

So why aren't we keeping it real? Why do we wear masks? We don't love our neighbors. We don't correct and train in love. When you speak to me, keep it real. Look me in the eye when you speak to me.

WHY DO WE LIE?

Why are we not forgiving and forgetting?
Why do we gossip?
Why are we not being honest with ourselves?
Are we keeping it real?
To thine own self be true.
Keep it REAL

WHY?

Why am I settling for less, when God wants to give me his best. Is it because I think less of God? Is it because I think less of me? Why? Why am I being so foolish? Why? Is it because I don't trust God? Is it because of me? I don't believe or is it because I don't know how to receive? Why can't I believe in me?

God says: "It will take some time, but you will believe and receive me!" **AMEN**

Choices:

I choose to rebel
When God chose to excel.
I thought it was about me but I was blind and couldn't see.
I wanted to hate but God stepped in through fate.
I have made a lot of bad choices in my life,
But I thank God for intervening in my strife.
Be Blessed
AMEN

Chapter Twenty

CHANGING ME

ANGELA POWELL

Changing Me

I have a history of domestic violence, post traumatic stress disorder, and I am an alcoholic. I never considered my kids feelings or thoughts during this time. They are very quiet like me so I always thought they were okay. Little did I know, they saw me at my worst for the last 10 years. I participated in parties at my friend's house and drove home after drinking with them in the car. My children listened to me yell at their father while I was intoxicated. They have witnessed me going from drunken rages to crying hysterically. All of these things happened to me; I still thought my kids were okay. How could they be when they worried if they were going to get home safely, or if the police would come during a fight?

My kids definitely have feelings. They wanted me to be happy. They wanted me to be a normal mother; they just wanted me to stop drinking!

They worry and are concerned just like any other human being. I love and cherish them enough to get help to stop. I want to include them on my road to recovery through Mary Hall Freedom House.

Chapter Twenty-One

WHAT WENT WRONG?

PONZETTA RICHMOND

What Went Wrong?

Before I started to write this I asked a lot of questions, "Renee where do I start? How much do I write?"

She told me, "what got you on the road of disaster to where you are now."

This has been a dream of mine for a long time. I would start writing, stop, move, lose the composition book, get tired, and just say, "forget it."

Scarlet had a favorite saying in the movie Gone with the Wind, "We will deal with that tomorrow."

That's the way my life was from the age of 16 to 40 years old. I didn't know how to deal with anything. I didn't know what my problem was. It was easy to deny it than face the truth. I went through that all the time. From 1st grade I couldn't remember anything the teacher said. Spacing out in class, being removed from my mind, everyone thought I didn't try hard but I did. There was no one to tell me what was wrong with me. My teacher had no education on learning disabilities. They just said I was stupid. No one noticed except my teachers, Mrs. Davis and Mrs. Anchor. They knew, but there were no classes to help in 1964. Why can't I remember to spell or do math like everyone else? I couldn't move forward. Maybe that's where my anger and shame began. I didn't want the teacher to call on me because I was afraid I might answer wrong. I didn't fit in, but I fit in everywhere else. All the things that would make me money when I got older, I fit in.

High school was great. I drove the school bus. My brother left a '72 Chevy at home when he went into the Army. Then he traded that for a 1975 brand new Cutlass. I was "big girl on campus" of Western Alamance. I had my happy moments in high school. I made sure when you looked at the yearbook of 1976, I'm everywhere. That was a good time. The camera made me feel beautiful. Even the principal told me "Ponz, no one is going to forget you." I may not have fit in or have been popular but I was in my yearbook. I still was happy but confused on what was wrong with my mind.

As the years went by, I moved to D.C. Lonely from the country, I didn't know anything. I was still a virgin and the girls were too fast, grown up, and doing whatever they wanted to do. They had no fathers or mothers to raise them. At 17 years old, I started smoking pot and drinking heavily. Doing whatever I wanted to do, thinking that it was good but it wasn't. Pot lead to Black Beauties and to Rum. My life was a mess. I was an alcoholic by the age of 23. I left D.C. and moved to Georgia in 1983 because my life had fallen apart.

It was rainy on that Greyhound November 16, 1983. I heard the song *Rainy Night in Georgia* pop into my head. Lonely, ashamed, and afraid, I wanted to give up but saying, " this is a new beginning" kept me going. And boy, it was a new beginning!

In 1999, Crack became my new friend. I didn't start crack because of peer pressure or to impress anyone; I started out of loneliness, boredom and depression. I didn't know I was depressed at the time. I wasn't hooked up with God. I had no trust and no faith. I would just walk alone, not talking or letting people know, just drinking every day. I thought me and crack could keep our little secret. " I won't tell if you don't tell," I told crack. But crack wasn't my friend and she told everyone. She told by the way I started looking. She told when she wouldn't let me keep money in my pocket. She told when I stopped paying rent. She told when I kept the lights on for 2 years. I gave up all the rest of my friends because I didn't want them to know I had another friend. Her name is Crack. No last name.

Living in Butler Park in Grady's home, I was back and forth to jail. Every time someone asked me if I was on drugs I said no. I was lying. It became easy for me because I was being a friend to Crack but she wasn't keeping our secret. She didn't play fair. She made me lose weight, made my skin turn all black; my hands looked like feet, just ugly. I used to travel, ride well, and go places. I went down hills and valleys until I just got tired. It took some years to come out of that grave. All I needed was the flower laid upon my chest, my soul was dead, but I was still saying, "I will deal with that tomorrow."

Today 2012, I can reach out and accept help. I'm capable of changing with my broken heart and crushed spirit. I still love a good challenge and sobriety is the biggest challenge of my life. So, y'all come on down to Mary Hall Freedom House and get yourself some of this stuff I have been receiving for 4 years. It was my choice to stay for 4 years because when I came in I would sit with my arms folded, saying "thank you Jesus". Now I'm up clapping my hands, saying "Thank You Jesus." Mrs. Lucy has a way of setting you up for the glory of God. When you call on the name of Jesus, he has the power to set you free.

Oh… I kicked Scarlet out of the door. I'm dealing with my life today.

Chapter Twenty-Two

LOST IN THE STREETS

TAMARA SANDERS

Lost in the Streets

My Story starts with me out in the streets doing just about everything under the sun that wasn't right for me. I was drinking heavily, smoking just about heavier, staying up some nights just to do it. One night while walking and drinking I got arrested for walking with an open container. Two weeks after I was in jail, I found out I was pregnant. Once I got out of jail, I tried my best to do the right thing.

My boyfriend and I got closer at this time. As long as I did the right thing it seemed we always did better, but still I was drawn to drugs and alcohol. With my baby in mind, I decided that I wanted true happiness. I made up my mind to get help. My boyfriend told me to try and see whom he sees. I thought about that for a few days. I came to call this place called Mary Hall Freedom House who would not only accept me pregnant but let me stay after the baby is born. I was so excited. I called, did all of the necessary work, and from my first call I had a bed on the fifth day. I was all right and I knew it. I feel like I will find real happiness and I will get a real chance. Thank you to all at MHFH.

Chapter Twenty-Three

Savina, Mommy is Sorry!

Patricia Taylor

Savina, Mommy is Sorry!

Dear Savina,

First of all let me say that I love you with every fiber of my being. You are the reason I get up every morning, my drive to keep going, and my inspiration.

I know I haven't been the perfect mother, I have made things very hard for the both of us. I have this thing called addiction, it has taken over my life for the past 12 years. I never thought about the damage I was doing to you until the damage was done.

When you were 16 months old I felt like my back was against the wall. I was homeless with no money, a child and no way out. I tried so hard to make life better for the both of us. I couldn't make ends meet. I eventually went back to the life I knew before you were born. I started selling myself to make sure you had what you needed. Little to my surprise, I was slowly dragging myself back into the pits of hell. I started going back around to the places I lived in my active addiction.

It wasn't long after that when I started using again. I thought I was doing the right thing by keeping you with me. Again, I didn't know the damage I was doing to you. I was so out of control. I never intended on you getting hurt. There was so many times I would leave you with Pop pop or anyone else who would keep you in order for me to go get high. I thought life was fine. More than once I had to get someone to come get you because I had to hide from tricks and dope dealers. Until one day I didn't get you away fast enough and I watched one of the worst nightmares ever. A gun was put to your head in order to get me out of the house. I still didn't stop. Baby girl, I was sick and knew no other way. Still thinking I was doing what was best by keeping you with me, it wasn't long after that the

Department of Children Services was called. You were taken away from me. That was by far the best thing that has ever happened to me. I then had the reality check I needed to get myself in order. God finally got my attention. I knew if I didn't stop and try His way of life that not only would I never see you again, but I would die in my life of sin. I had to change, and it was time for me to do some serious footwork.

I finally surrendered; I hit my knees and begged for mercy. I couldn't live without you. God gave me the power and strength I needed. The pain I saw in your eyes everyday was more than enough to keep me in line. Savina, you are the love of my life, I never meant to hurt you or to put you in danger. I couldn't see past the drugs. I never stopped loving you or fighting for you and I never will. The day will come when we will be together again. Once this program is completed you will be home. I promise to love you and protect you from this day forward. You will never have to see the hell you saw before. Please forgive me for the things that I did in my addiction. I'm Sorry My Lil Sunshine. Mommy Loves You!

Love always,

Mommy

Chapter Twenty-Four

GRASP THE SOURCE

ALISHA J. THOMAS

Grasp the Source

Life Alert; "I've fallen and I can't get Up!"
Uncontrollable downward spiral
Bottomless pit so it seems; dreams with no seams
Streams of tears – NIGHTMARE!
Does anyone care?
(Overwhelmed with fear)
Does anyone hear my wretched, heartbreaking cry? Am I
still alive?
Hello? Hello? HELLO?!
Uncomfortable silence
(Thief in the night with his overly zealous missions:
To STEAL, KILL, and DESTROY.
Demons wring their hands, transparently prideful while
obtaining eyefuls of pain, guilt, and sorrow; preparing for
morrow.)

Anger at self for almost admitting complete defeat.
Beat.
Scatter brain questions invade…
"Why, Why, WHY?!"
"Woe is me, Woe is me, oh pitiful me..."
—and—
All of a sudden... *I am*… "Huh?"...*I AM*… "What?"
(In the dark abysmal appears a single star off in the distance and in an instant a seed of hope enters and is planted.)
Demons gnash their teeth tugging at the skirt of the soul.
An opposite pull is noticed.
"I can't… I can't… I used, I abused, I was mean, and I was
obscene…
I judged, I cheated,
Lied, stole,
I was on hell's honor roll!"
(The Light grew)

I am here, I am yours and you are mine – I Love <u>You</u>.
"But I'm not worthy...But, but...I don't wanna die.
I know you, I created you
(Light casted out darkness; still the demons remained in
the shadows)
Have faith my Child – Just Believe, Believe that I AM.
"Look at my mess, I'm dirty and worn, my heart is torn,
and I don't think I can manage another storm."
Child, don't you know that I see you!
I SEE YOU, I hear you. Your value has never dwindled.
Don't you know that I am your Father, that I am the King
of kings!
You are my Child, and heir, you are royalty.
Take you place—dominion over my creations on earth.
Stop listening to lies, dry you eyes—you are forgiven,
Forgive yourself!
Execute my mission, armor yourself, we must engage in
this supernatural war.
Battle after battle we must FIGHT!
Get Up!
GET UP!
WE ARE VICTORS!
Think for a change.
Rearrange negatives to positives.
Resist and remain, stop the blame, don't be the same.
No more endless merry-go-rounds; we want triumphant
sounds
The time in now:
LIVE or DIE
Open your eyes. Enjoy His Creations, enjoy your life it is
a gift
Don't let time drift
Reason Season, no tit for tat; take hold, gain control
LOVE
Simple as that.
L.O.V.E.
Love God
Love you, Love me, LOVE

Chapter Twenty-Five

OLD REFLECTIONS

NATALIE VOLLES

Old Reflections

My reflection fades away
I am my own worst enemy
I don't know who I am
I'm lost
Sanity gone
Days passing by
Time is ticking
I'm still here
Still stuck
Poison runs through my veins
Tears flow from my eyes
Why am I still alive?
I cried out to God
Confusion and fear
Anger and hatred
My emotions overwhelm me
Help me Lord!
There seems no way out
Abandoned by so called friends
I pushed my family away
Its came down to God and me
He can heal my hurts
I just have to let him in
Give it all to God
I fall and he picks me up
He shines his light upon me in the darkness
My broken heart is healed
He fills my heart with love
Where do I go from here?
I'm still afraid to step forward
Afraid I will fail
This is all so unfamiliar
Unfamiliar ground

Starting over
So it's came down to this
I'm at the starting line
I've finally surrendered
I've accepted
I've became willing
My heart beats faster
Butterflies in my stomach
I'm scared to death
I'm learning how to live
Learning how to sleep
Learning how to laugh
Learning how to love
I'm learning
The word gives me peace
Even if only for one second,
It is still peace
I start to talk to God more and more
He understands me
He understands my hurts, my past, and still loves me
unconditionally
He is my provider
My father
My friend
My everything
He teaches me about recovery through the scriptures
I've started the steps
I'm learning the tools
I can cope today
I have come to believe that God can restore me to sanity
I walk the path He has lead for me to walk today
I no longer run in the opposite direction

PSALM 94:18

I cried out, "I am slipping!" But your unfailing love, O Lord,
supported me

From Falls To Freedom

I dig deep inside myself
To clear the trash of my past
I talk, I cry, I remember
The scars I have remind me where I came from
I never have to go back there again
A second of freedom is worth more than a lifetime of bondage
I dance in the rain
Sing in the shower
Lay in the sunshine
Listen to the wind blow
Gaze at the starry night
Life's beautiful moments
My heart fills with love and peace from God
The prison walls I built around myself have been broken
I am no longer a slave of my own decisions
I am a princess of God
I am free

Through his Eyes

Beautiful blue sparkling eyes
gaze at the new world around him
he doesn't even know he's a miracle
he withstood living in abandon houses
he had no say about the drugs running through his womb
he was around strangers, bad influences
he was out in the cold night
he kicked and kicked, trying to get out
of the place his mommy put him.

He is my Inspiration

Going through the bad but still coming into
This world strong.
God held his hand

And made him healthy

Thank you Lord

He opened my eyes to how I should be.
A love that's never ending.
Life comes and to take it with a smile
Despite what I had put him through he still loves me.
Now I have the chance to be the mom
I want to be to him
A new clean life with lots of love

Chapter Twenty-Six

POETIC JUSTICE

BRENDA WILLIAMSON

Poetic Justice

"The Wayfarer" by Stephen Crane

The wayfarer, perceiving the pathway to truth, was struck with astonishment. It was thickly grown with weeds. "Ha", he said, "I see that none has passed here, in a long time." Later he saw that each week was a singular knife. "Well," he mumbled at last, "doubtless there are other roads."

"Analysis of the Wayfarer" by Josefina

It is a poem about a person that is seeking the truth but, he realizes that to reach this he needs to endure many challenges and that not many take up this road to truth. At this thought he remembers that there are other roads, which while not being the way to truth, are much easier. He decides to take the easy way out, meaning that he will never really reach his truth.

I have learned that everything is different between our addiction and our recovery. Even in our subconscious, this is our dreams, feelings and our own thoughts.

"My Peaceful Day"

By Brenda Williamson

The day that I met you was the most glory full day. Now, I have a wonderful place to be when it is my time. When I do finally come to be with you, the beautiful colors I will see when I am there. My eyes will open, my heart is yours. Now I am at peace with myself and you. I love this love I have.

MY LITTLE SMILE

The small little face gleams in the sunlight, which makes your beautiful little smile glow. You look at me with a smile and a little giggle slips out from you, because of your happiness. My happiness in all the world is you.

This is dedicated to my daughter
Shelbi Madison LeMay
1998-2001

NEW SCHOOL PRAYER
"2001"

Now I sit me down in school where praying is against the rule. For this great nation under God, finds mention of him very odd. If scripture now the class recited, it violates the Bill of Rights. And anytime my head I bow becomes a Federal matter now. Our hair can be purple, orange, or green. That is no offense, it's a freedom scene. The law is specific, the law is precise. Prayers spoken aloud are a serious vice for praying in a public hall, might offend someone with no faith at all.

In silence alone we must meditate. God's name is prohibited by the state. We're allowed to cuss and dress like freaks and pierce our noses, tongues and cheeks. They have outlawed guns, but first the Bible. To quote the Good Book makes me liable. We can elect a pregnant girl "Senior Queen" and the "unwed daddy" our Senior King. It's "inappropriate" to teach right from wrong, we are taught such "Judgments" do not belong. We can get our condoms and birth control, study witchcraft, vampires and totem poles. But the Ten Commandments are not allowed. No word of must reach this crowd. It is scary here, I must confess, when chaos reigns the schools is a mess.

So Lord this silent plea I make should I be shot my soul please take.

Prayer written by my Aunt

"If you are ashamed of me, I will be ashamed of you before my Father!"

Chapter Twenty-Seven

TO MY SON WHO IS
MY INSPIRATION TO LIFE

KRISTIN WILLIAMSON

To My Son
Who Is My Inspiration to Life

TRISTAN BLAYK

You are the reason I love waking up each and every
morning. You brighten my world with your beautiful smile
along the way.
We've been down long curvy roads together.
You are my pride and joy so those are the last.
I'm going to make sure that I grow from the past.
As long as we keep God in our hearts,
He'll give us a whole new beginning of the beginning,
And we'll get a brand new start.
There's nothing like a child's love.
So I'm making this promise to you,
To stay clean and sober so you never have to feel like you're
Missing out on a mother's love.
You are my inspiration, my world, and my blood.
You need your mother to help you grow tall,
And God's making it happen, Thanks to Mary Hall.

Love, Mommy

Conclusion

MY STEPS

Yes, my steps are ordered, this I know for the Bible tells me so. Often times women want to know their purpose, their destiny, the plan, I tell women all the time two things. First, it's assuring to know that we all have a purpose in being on this earth, and second, I am so glad I know that all things are working for my good.

When I had accomplished 7 years in recovery, God called me to Atlanta, Georgia to begin a work in me, after bringing me out of the darkness of addiction. The Lord used my strengths in being able to help others by loving them and sharing my experience, strength and hope. I tell women daily "I will love you until you learn to love yourself".

I grew up in a little village in Westchester, New York, called Tuckahoe. My mom died when I was six years old from alcoholism. Growing up I never knew I was living in the projects, which was considered not a good place to live, and that drinking and getting high wasn't a normal way of life. By the time I realized the negative impact that both drugs and alcohol can have on one's life, it seemed as if it was too late for me. I was already out of the projects and I was in full-blown addiction.

I hit bottom when I was told, "I had the right to remain silent". I couldn't imagine being silent, or not being free. Life wasn't in sync for me quite yet, there was a greater plan. I cried out to God and turned my will and life over and yes, I am amazed every day that He saved me, and He gave me direction, because I wanted nothing more than to give my life to Him for His divine purpose in my life.

I am fulfilled and blessed when I bring light and hope to people in darkness and despair, and I know that it truly blesses the Lord. Miracles happen every day at Mary Hall Freedom House. How can you not believe there is a God? Your Momma couldn't help you, your baby daddy couldn't save you, and parole took away your freedom. God heard your prayers and said, "I know the plans I have for you", Jeremiah 29:11. Give it up, and over to God and the journey of recovery will be amazing not only for you, but for all who God will bring into your life.

Your steps are ordered, just wait and see. What He has done for me He will surely do for you. Your journey awaits you. Embrace the only one that will never leave you nor forsaken you, and you will see the very essence of His presence in your life!

FROM THE HEART OF LUCY HALL

I LOVE YOU!